FAST CARS

chevrolet
CORVETTE

by Lisa Bullard

Reading Consultant:
Barbara J. Fox
Reading Specialist
North Carolina State University

Content Consultant:
James Elliott
Editor
Classic & Sports Car magazine

Capstone
press

Mankato, Minnesota

Blazers is published by Capstone Press,
151 Good Counsel Drive, P.O. Box 669, Mankato, Minnesota 56002.
www.capstonepress.com

Library of Congress Cataloging-in-Publication Data
Bullard, Lisa.
    Chevrolet Corvette / by Lisa Bullard.
    p. cm. —(Blazers. Fast cars)
    Includes bibliographical references and index.
    ISBN-13: 978-1-4296-0098-9 (hardcover)
    ISBN-10: 1-4296-0098-5 (hardcover)
    1. Corvette automobile—Juvenile literature. I. Title.
TL215.C6B85 2008
629.222'2—dc22   2006102216

Summary: Briefly describes the history and models of the Chevrolet Corvette.

Editorial Credits
Erika L. Shores, editor; Bobbi J. Wyss, designer; Jo Miller, photo researcher

Photo Credits
Alamy/Isadora Poggi Photography, 7; Transtock, Inc./Guy Spangenberg, 15 (top),
    16–17, 20–21
Corbis/Bettmann, 6, 14 (bottom); Reuters/Lucas Jackson, 28–29
Ron Kimball Stock/Rom Kimball, 8–9, 12, 13, 15 (bottom), 18–19, 27
Shutterstock/Drazen Vukelic, 24–25; hfng's Gallery, cover
ZUMA Press/Action Press, 22–23; General Motors, 10–11, 14 (top); Harvey
    Schwartz, 4–5, 26

Essential content terms are **bold** and are defined at the bottom of the page where
they first appear.

1 2 3 4 5 6 12 11 10 09 08 07

TABLE OF CONTENTS

chapter 1

AMERICA'S SPORTS CAR

Vroom! A Chevrolet Corvette zooms around the corner. Every head turns to watch America's famous sports car.

Chevrolet was the first big American carmaker to build a sports car. Today, Corvettes eat up roads and racetracks around the world.

First Corvettes roll off assembly line in 1953.

fast fact

All of the first Corvettes were convertibles.

chapter 2

FIFTY FANTASTIC YEARS

Chevrolet introduced the Corvette in 1953. People were surprised to see a sports car made in the United States instead of Europe.

fast fact

Corvettes are named after a type of warship.

Over the years, Corvettes changed with each new *model*. In 1955, Chevrolet added a new V8 engine. The 1963 Corvette Sting Ray had a split rear window.

model — the new design of a car that comes out each year

1971 Chevrolet Corvette Stingray

In 1965, Chevrolet added a more
powerful engine. Fewer changes were
made to the 1970s and 1980s Corvettes.
In the 1990s, the ZR-1 model made
Corvette a speed king again.

fast fact

Chevrolet has built more than 1.3 million Corvettes since 1953.

003770

1993 ZR-1 Chevrolet Corvette

CORVETTE TIMELINE

Corvette Sting Ray released.

1963

1953

1977

The 500,000th Corvette is made.

Chevrolet introduces the Corvette.

The newest Corvettes are the sixth generation of America's sports car. The C6 hit the road as the 2005 model.

The Z06 Corvette is released.

2001

1989

1997

The C5 Corvette is released.

ZR-1 Corvette introduced.

chapter 3

HIGH PERFORMANCE

New Corvettes perform better than ever before. Larger brakes and bigger wheels give drivers more control around corners.

The newest Corvettes are faster and smaller. Chevrolet changed their shape to make them more *aerodynamic*.

> **aerodynamic** —
> **built to move easily**
> **through the air**

fast fact

Corvette designers build full-size models out of clay to see how their ideas will look.

The 2006 Corvette Z06 is faster than any earlier **_production_** Corvette. Its 505-horsepower V8 engine has a top speed of nearly 200 miles (322 km) per hour.

production — describes
a vehicle produced for
mass-market sale

CORVETTE DIAGRAM

hood

high-intensity headlamp

hood ornament

bumper

FERRARI

CORVETTE

raked windshield

alloy wheel

chapter 4

TRENDSETTER

Corvettes are made with cutting-edge materials. Corvettes have light *fiberglass* bodies. Parts of the Z06 engine are made of titanium, a strong, lightweight metal.

fiberglass — a strong, lightweight material made from thin threads of glass

New Corvettes feature the Head-Up Display system. It shows gauge information on the windshield. Drivers don't need to look down to see their speed.

Head-Up Display system

fast fact

Corvette owners really love their cars. One owner was even buried in his Corvette.

chapter 5

LOOKING AHEAD

Future Corvette designs are top secret, but one thing seems sure. The next generation of America's sports car will be one of the world's supercars.

GLOSSARY

aerodynamic (air-oh-dye-NAM-mik)—built to move easily through the air

convertible (kuhn-VUR-tuh-buhl)—a car with a top that can be lowered or removed

fiberglass (FYE-bur-glass)—a strong, lightweight material made from thin threads of glass

gauge (GAYJ)—a dial or instrument used to measure something, such as an engine's temperature

generation (jen-uh-RAY-shuhn)—a way to classify cars that were made within a certain group of years and have common design elements

model (MOD-uhl)—the new design of a car that comes out each year

performance (pur-FOR-muhnss)—a car's ability to achieve speed, power, and handling

production (pruh-DUHK-shuhn)—describes a vehicle produced for mass-market sale

EAD MORE

Hawley, Rebecca. *Corvette.* Superfast Cars.
New York: PowerKids Press, 2007.

Kimber, David. *Auto-Mania!* Vehicle-Mania!
Milwaukee: Gareth Stevens, 2004.

Stacy, Lee. *Corvette.* Hot Cars. Vero Beach, Fla.:
Rourke, 2005.

NTERNET SITES

FactHound offers a safe, fun way
to find Internet sites related
to this book. All of the sites
on FactHound have been
researched by our staff.

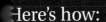

Here's how:
1. Visit *www.facthound.com*
2. Choose your grade level.
3. Type in this book ID **1429600985** for
   age-appropriate sites. You may also
   browse subjects by clicking on letters,
   or by clicking on pictures and words.
4. Click on the **Fetch It** button.

FactHound will fetch the best sites for you!

INDEX